VELD FIRES

First published in 2024 by
The Dedalus Press
13 Moyclare Road
Baldoyle
Dublin D13 K1C2
Ireland

www.dedaluspress.com

ISBN 978-1-915629-29-6 (paperback)
ISBN 978-1-915629-28-9 (hardback)

Dedalus Press titles are available in Ireland
from Argosy Books (www.argosybooks.ie) and in the UK
from Inpress Books (www.inpressbooks.co.uk).

Cover painting: 'Big Sky' by Daryl Nero,
by kind permission of the artist's estate.

Dedalus Press receives financial assistance from
The Arts Council / An Chomhairle Ealaíon.

VELD FIRES

JOSEPH WOODS

DEDALUS PRESS

Acknowledgements

This book has been enabled through generous grants from the Katherine & Patrick Kavanagh fellowship and the Arts Council of Ireland and for which the author is sincerely grateful.

Some of these poems or versions of them have appeared in the following: *Metamorphic, 21st century poets respond to Ovid,* eds Paul Munden & Nessa O'Mahony (Recent Work Press, Canberra, Australia, 2017); *Cuban Love Songs,* ed. Ronan Sheehan (Cassandra Voices, Dublin, 2020); *I am a man of peace: writings inspired by the Maynooth University Ken Saro-Wiwa Collection,* ed. Helen Fallon (Daraja Press, Wakefield, Canada, 2020); *Pestilence,* eds. Peter Pegnall & Gérard Noyau (Lapwing Publications, Belfast 2020); *Divining Dante,* eds. Paul Munden & Nessa O'Mahony (Recent Work Press, Canberra, Australia, 2021); *Days of Clear Light, A Festschrift in honour of Jessie Lendennie & in celebration of Salmon Poetry at 40,* eds. Alan Hayes & Nessa O'Mahony (Salmon Poetry, County Clare, 2021); *Local Wonders: Poems of our Immediate Surrounds,* ed. Pat Boran (Dedalus Press, Dublin, 2021); *Romance Options, Love Poems for Today,* eds. Leeanne Quinn & Joseph Woods (Dedalus Press, Dublin, 2022). 'Memory Swallows' and 'Firey-necked Nightjar' were broadcast on the Poetry File, Evelyn Grant's Weekend Drive, RTÉ Lyric FM, 2021. Poems were also published in *Cyphers, The Irish Times, The Ogham Stone 2023 & Temenos Academy Review.*

'Firey-necked Nightjar' was put to music for electric jazz guitar in a composition by Matt Greenwood and performed in the Vanilla Moon, Harare.

Sincere thanks to Pat Boran for his always astute editing and support.

Contents

~

Mornington / 9

for the house of the planter is known by the trees / 10

At Christmas Pass / 11

Golden Valley, Rangoon, Remembered / 12

Three / 13

The Shipping News / 14

Bulawayo Train Station / 15

African Night Train / 16

Cave Paintings / 18

Muizenberg, New Year's Eve / 19

American Club, Rangoon / 20

Game Drive / 21

Fiery-necked Nightjar / 22

Cholera / 24

Summerhouse / 25

the warden had not opened just for me / 26

Ireland: A Terrible Beauty / 28

Great Zimbabwe / 30

To be in Lüderitz / 31

Memory Swallows / 33

The Pillars of the House / 34

Quarantine / 35

Ambrosia / 36

Derrynaflan / 37

Roadside Shrine / 38

Other Families' Ghosts / 39

Wheatear / 40

Most Appealing Eyes / 41

Punch Rock / 43

An Achill Island Icon / 44

Sunshine / 45

Vides ut alta / 46

Found Poem/Poet / 47

Hoist sails and gather the scorching gulf winds / 48

Fireflies / 51

French Toast / 53

A Ford Prefect in Franschhoek / 54

An African Hoopoe for Derek Mahon / 55

At Altamont / 56

The dream of home from a great distance / 57

Let's get lost / 59

Rain Storks / 60

Bicycle Thieves / 61

Summer Home Fires Burning / 62

Distant Accordion Music / 64

Are you a farmer? / 65

Egg-fried Rice / 66

Islander / 67

Kermanshah / 68

Keenagh / 70

Enough to get us to Marondera / 71

Boxed Set / 72

Corncrake / 73

⌒

NOTES / 74

for Sarah and Eliza,
journeywomen of my life

⁀

What of the season of veld fires, which had a
climate of its own: lowering, smoky horizons,
the yellow thickness of the middle air, the black
wastes of veld? It was an extra season inserted
into the natural year.

— *Martha Quest,* Doris Lessing

Mornington

Ten days after mother died
it was time to turn for home
and in prep for Zimbabwe's
land-locked vistas, a last walk
on the beach where, behind
its dunes, you lingered
your last few years
in a home for the elderly
having lost all interest …

A buoy bobs
in front of a shipwreck
that's been rusting and sinking
into these sands, all my life.

A ship waits on the horizon
with lights on in daylight
and a great world of work
going on within, prone
for the pilot to guide it
through estuarine shallows
and then upriver, the narrow deep
to my home town.

So often the bridges
and flags of those great ships
disappearing behind sand dunes,
Suez of my childhood.

for the house of the planter is known by the trees

—*Austin Clarke*

Sweet suburbs of Harare
and bungalows that are known
by the trees, parades of purple
jacarandas, poinsettias and flame trees
and, beyond their boundaries,

the swards of green
edging to the road with sprinklers
levitating even in dry season.
And the sweeping, swish sweeping
by liveried gardeners always in blue

who bid 'baas' or 'sir'
to my passing 'good morning'
or who pause and chat among
themselves in front of compounds
whose walls are topped

with sometimes sizzling wires
and unforgiving electric gates
that snap shut after a glimpse
of the interior. Every avenue
looks the same, and were it not

for the colour of ornamental trees
you could get lost among the reassuringly
foreign street names: Sandringham, Churchill, Windsor …

At Christmas Pass

for Irene Staunton

A tree at the toll gate
before Christmas Pass
and the ascent

then corkscrew descent
into Mutare,
and that tree decorated

with Weaver bird nests
swaying in the sultry wind,
baubles on a Christmas tree.

Golden Valley, Rangoon, Remembered

i

Brutalist 1950s-style villa
provenance 1960s regime
now empty and baked
into decrepitude
while the elderly staff sit it out
in a shack at the back,
their bosses having left
for the new capital.

ii

Disconsolately,
the red-whiskered bulbul
hops and pecks among
the scattered putrefying guavas,
windfalls or rainfalls?

Three

Me and my recently three
year-old daughter
having horseplay

on the bed
under the dome
of a mosquito net

when inevitably
we bash our heads
and there's tears.

I go get ice,
direct its glide
across her temple,

kiss to make
it better but smart
at her cold flesh.

Three days after
she came into this world,
I kissed my father's marble forehead.

The Shipping News

Religiously, I listen to the 5.20 am Shipping Forecast,
where it's one hour later here and time to get up,
and whose soothing placename litany
charms me from sleep, and adrift
in my Southern Hemisphere, land–locked fug.

Bulawayo Train Station

Toddler Eliza points out an oil spillage
long dried up on the deserted platform
and asks, what is it?
'Oil.'
'I know a gate in Burma
that could do with that.'

African Night Train

Pretty much all that is left of you, uncle;
an en route postcard from Nairobi,
a letter in copperplate from Lusaka in '59
and two photos which I brought out with me.

Oh, and a monochrome painting of
a distant naked woman standing and punting
a dug-out canoe, in the Okavango perhaps?
Which you bought or bartered

from a fellow prisoner, or so the family
legend goes, and now hanging
in my sister's home in Meath.
This was your life, a passing through

of places, encounters like the one in the photo,
you and some guy fishing at a named
Rhodesian dam I've never located.
Along with my siblings we'll be the last

to remember you. I thought in Zim
I'd find some clue, but even archives hold
their secrets sometimes. From the picture
of you in your railway chummery at Broken Hill,

I see your brazen scowl, that's matched in me.
Guard of the goods train with the bonus
of your own cabin and a storm lamp
swaying in the wake of an African night.

Loneliness was your second skin,
a Diogenes who eventually returned.
Once, my father brought home a bundle
of books from the long defunct

Railway Lending Library and among them
the leather-bound and aromatic *Lion Hunting*
in gold tooling, which, on one of your rare visits,
you lit upon and defaced in blue biro

with my name and address, *5 Railway Terrace,*
then read passages in your mock colonial
accent, for far too long for it to be funny.

Cave Paintings

Helping my daughter dress
she asks me about the lines
on her belly.
'Sleep creases?' I suggest.
'They look like cave paintings to me.'

Muizenberg, New Year's Eve

A last stroll up the coast from Muizenberg to St Georges
on a stretch that always reminds me of seaside Bray back home,
and not a soul to be seen and the wind wildly up. A Cessna
struggles like a cormorant across False Bay but breaks through.
I turn at Rhodes' Cottage where, in the front room on a stifling
March evening, he breathed his last. This morning I lingered
in that room, ambivalent, and aware, just shy of fifty, he was
    younger
than me. And how they kept to the letter of his will, the corpse
to its own personal carriage and train, sent north to sacred Matopos.
Interred in a granite whaleback among gigantic boulders, a tomb
bearing no epitaph, having had the country named after him.

American Club, Rangoon

Dad and daughter
at the club
on a tropically empty
weekday.

I push the swing to
'again, again, again'
and stare through
the wired-off lake

to a man fishing
who waves over,
and warily I wave
back. We swim

in the recently
re-tiled pool
as refreshing,
in this heat

as warm soup,
and I float face up
to the sun while
you recall some epic

family event
from your four years.
'Well, you have a great memory,'
and you reply
'Some of it is in my body.'

Game Drive

Our daughter grows bored on the game drive -
we've been out all day in a jeep and my bird list
bolsters while the sun seems to grow, shifting
to setting mode. So many hippos gathered
on the water's edge, common as beetles and even
beetle-like in the distance. And the woolly-necked
stork who has just descended has been renamed
a 'stinky-necked stork' after the close-up of the
ghoulish Marabou earlier this morning. And elephants,
numerous as sheep on your uncle's farm last Christmas,
and then one silhouette of a truly enormous specimen
like something from that movie you've watched over and over.
You are hungry now and longing for the fish you caught
this morning, your first ever, one on each line
of your first six casts. And just as we are turning
from the water's edge, the adults unfairly fortified with gin,
we see two lionesses, on a slope facing the sun, like our own cats
back in Harare. Mercifully for our daughter at least,
a zebra kill has been concealed behind bushes while a lion cub pokes
its head out, to gawk at us. Complete, and speedily home now
through long shadows of bush veld, we have the lake to cross
to our island named after a kind of goose, in an open motor boat,
the sky turned navy and the lights of old approaching
while avoiding poles of dead trees spectrally rising
from the water, when she shouts,
'Look, look over there, *a rabbit.*'

Fiery-necked Nightjar

i.m. Macdara Woods

There it sings again, Macdara,
heralding dusk in the lull before
the orchestration of the southern
African night, a song I'll indelibly
associate with you,
though I never got to tell you
but do now, and since you didn't distinguish
between the living and the dead.

And not that your last years
should define you; those interminable
confinements and hospital stays
which you turned into your own
personal Magic Mountain
and worked through,
disentangling those dimensions,
exercised in the still night …

Lazarus-like, you took flight
and travelled further and faster
than the rest of us, above dark
ancestral Meath and north
to the Russian steppes,
conjugating their verbs.

Then I was settling into the outskirts
of Harare, an African *rus in urbe*
– and not Harar which you once
mistakenly elevated it to, where one
of your immortals, still ghosts –

and often up late reading under the house
creaks, turning over one of your telegrams
while outside that nocturnal singer of fire
would punctuate.

Litany bird or 'Goat milker' from the Latin,
erroneous and thus assumed for its secretive ways.
Glimpsed only once when its descending
and quavering call drew me outside
on one of those immense moonlit nights
to see its silhouette on a wire, flicker and go.
Toddlers abed have been known to hum
its call long before they can talk.

Litany bird, I hear it just now
repeating its refrain:
Good Lord, deliver us ...
Good Lord, deliver us ...

Cholera

No sooner had the President been sworn in
when cholera stalked the high-density
neighbourhoods of the capital
and, with medieval aplomb
scythed a score and more.
An early act of grace by the President
was to pay passage for the former First Lady
and adversary, to attend her mother's funeral.
Five thousand air-miles in a private jet, whose luxury
she announced on return, had helped soften the blow.
In the suburbs, jacarandas arched to meet over avenues,
their purpling begun and soon snowfalls of sticky petals,
while emerald-green verges glistened
to the furious flinching of water-sprinklers.

Summerhouse

Tumbleweed of fluff, hair and dust
caught in the corner of our attic bedroom.
Daintily, I let it roll out the Velux window
to disappear like a soap bubble,
something of us in its sphere.

the warden had not opened just for me

Sugar loaf mountains and a few with ski slopes, when it grew dark
and each station seemed submerged with snow and then night.
For much of the four-and-a-half-hour train journey whose sum
would not deliver me to my destination, I slept, studied maps,

dipped into Pascal and revised phrases, while a middle-aged man
across the aisle flicked lazily through a *manga* and a young woman
squirmed beside him, or so I remember it.

At my stop, the now relentless rain bulleted holes in the snow,
I took a taxi to the hostel on the hill, in the hope that, out of season,
it might still be open. As we neared the top, I imagined the driver
politely explaining it was closed. The road ended in a quagmire

and the hostel in darkness, despite the early hour of eight
or thereabouts. Around the building, I went searching:
only dim interior lights, a show for security and little else.
While the taxi waited, I grew wet.

No one answered until the shape of a man moved across
and I tapped the window. Cautiously, he came to the door
and showed me a dorm, and then I was eating a bowl of ramen
in what appeared to be his quarters, while further on in the hostel

he ran an *ofuro* for me. Speaking no English, he mustered
    'April Fool'
when I wrote the date in the ledger, in the hall stacked with skis.
After bathing I choose a lower bunk and was soon sound asleep.

To be awoken by people noisily arriving in heavy boots
and clattering skis, muttering in Japanese. During this carry on,
snow flumped from the roof and was interrupted, I was sure,
by an outrageous ringing of the reception bell. I slipped back
    to sleep,

consoled that the warden had not opened just for me.
Summoned for breakfast that morning and before reaching
the bottom of the stairs, strains of Vivaldi's 'The Four Seasons'

loudly announced my arrival in the sun-lit hall. My place set in
    the middle
of a narrow table, and the lady reassured me I was last night's
    only guest.
Left alone, I looked out on a landscape thawing, when an Arctic fox
slinked by, its coat already turning to patches of yellow.

Spring was presenting, even here, and with no one about
I left a Thank You note and cash at reception and set off,
the journey to the frozen sea ahead of me.

Ireland: A Terrible Beauty

'Although they are not a physically beautiful people,
I found it easy to make beautiful pictures of them.'
— Jill Uris

The front cover a study in grey and eggshell blue,
it has been raining for days, for weeks perhaps
with absolutely no let up, and now the mist
has lowered in twilight, quenching the last light
and folds of mountains. Call it a crossroads
but more of a T-junction brokering nowhere,
and unmistakably the west for this ratcheting
of bleakness. A ruined house backs onto the mountain

and, by its gable, a signpost proclaims a few
indecipherable townlands or villages and probably
points in the wrong direction; mischievously
switched in that one summer of mirth and laughter
that no one alive recalls. A coffee table book
of unintended Gothic, from the front to the back
cover portrait of a Belfast child, whose curled
lip and furious fish eyes, topped by a martial cap,

would trouble the physiognomist's long night.
I remember the book from childhood library visits,
top shelf and invariably face-out as if to shame us all
in its portrayal of benign Irish misery.
Now my second-hand edition, inscribed,
'Eastlea, Salisbury, Rhodesia, Africa, 1977,'
subscribes to a vintage of another sort …

But back to the dog stood in the middle of the road,
one stinky eye sizing up the photographer,
the other on a heavily stooped old man in black
from his wellingtons to his cap, but determined
to the eggshell blue building which has something
of the demeanour of a shop about it. Proclaiming
nothing, not even a name above its door, and the same
old man, on an errand eternally for bread and bacon.

Great Zimbabwe

Home from Zimbabwe for the holidays
and at a family gathering, I usher your six-
year-old-self into the hall, and toward
a Mo Irwin masterpiece,
Hope, The Chapel of High Island 7/25
and ask what you think of it,
and you knowingly nod and say,
'Ah yes, *Great Zimbabwe.*'

To be in Lüderitz

Ludicrous to be in Lüderitz
after days driving through the desert
where the only sign of life
is wildlife or occasionally
the glint of a solitary steel
windmill churning light
in the distance
marking a farm far off
or where someone once
farmed, and abandoned
railway stations connecting
to a mostly concealed narrow-gauge
whose mystery must be;
who in the desert they ever served?
And now to find myself
at the top of a hill
with my back to the narrow
Lutheran church and looking
down on the town and a full
street of colonial German
houses running to the sea
and Shark Island, really a peninsula
and where later we'll collect
sea glass washed up in the sand,
shards that have lost their sharpness
from being buffed around
on the shingle shore to the sea floor
and back again. Bring them home,
yes, in a Ziplock bag
along with pouches
of Egg-timer desert sand, bone white
to ochre red, and in jars we'll arrange

on the window sill and not worry
about their fading since they
have seen more sun than we
can ever show them.

Memory Swallows

Unexpectedly home from southern Africa in April
and you brightly recall your father, seven years gone,
and his annual startlement at how that swallow
would bolt from the blue, whizzing past the yard's belfry
and straight up the stone stairs like a guided missile
turning sharp right to the potting room, half-open
to the elements, and reconnoitring before rebuilding.

The Pillars of the House

You can live in a breeze-block bungalow
of 1970s vintage with an unpunctuated sign,
No trespassers our dogs will attack
in the window and where all the mismatched
and multi-coloured curtains are drawn.

You can live in a house where the gable was once
half-painted as high as an arm could reach
some summers ago – that have since accumulated –
and the job abandoned for some other botherment.

You can live in a house where the anarchy
of the front garden includes a carved pier-head
surplus to requirements and remaindered
on a pallet at sea in an ocean of moss.

You can live in a house where towers of firewood
ample for ten severe winters, engulf the rear
garden and roll over the perimeter wall
to an open field like an unstoppable tide.

You can live in a house where oddly proportioned
Corinthian columns you could never live up to,
uphold a flimsy porch, consoled that no one
will ever trouble your door for directions.

You can live in virtuous isolation, in a safe house
in national lockdown, content the cattle grid
will never rattle the announcement of new arrivals.

Quarantine

i.m. Eavan Boland

From the frying pan and hopefully not into the fire
we travelled six thousand miles, and at Addis Ababa
saw queues for China and people dressed as astronauts
hermetically sealed for the journey home, back to the epicentre
which had already shifted direction toward ours.

Perhaps, ill-advisedly, we sipped beer in the 'London Bar'
and watched it all pass when our daughter welled up
at the incongruity of it all, spacesuits passing
in front of us and screens to the right and left of us,
streaming horror headlines.

My lungs being heavy, we exchanged the *cordon sanitaire*
of our compound, the veranda, heat and high altitude of Harare,
for the loan of a gate-lodge on the family farm – built in Black '47
but more Wordsworthian now in its yellow wash and waiting
    wisteria,
a spell in rural rectitude and cold-comfort Ireland, but the beacon

of home strengthening. The clocks obligingly went back the weekend
of our arrival, but dawns are grey and the lengthening evenings
hold no heat. I hog the fire and the cold outside is freighted
    with fear,
blood thinned by a near decade in the tropics. The demesne trees
are towering spectres of leaflessness, and up on the hill

the only colour in rows of planted ash is the flicker of gold
in the wing of a finch. I look down upon a great quilt of fields,
and even the land has taken on a *verboten* feel,
I might as well be staring upon the ice sheets of Antarctica.

Ambrosia

Nothing was done since
with the bachelor's bungalow,
and the overgrown front garden
has a handful of fertiliser bags
upended with spewed empty tins
of blue Ambrosia Creamed Rice,
the dyspeptic's choice.

Derrynaflan

for Rosita Boland

A buzzard over Ballyowen when I set out from Dualla
to Derrynaflan during lockdown, stravaging the roads
like an emissary monk intent from Cashel.
Beyond Ballinure, a sense of the west widening, apparition
of stone walls and good land lowering to bad, a bog basin
stretched to eternity. After cavernous wet lanes,
a Mohican causeway over black peat led to a contour of green,
an island rising to a ruinous church and, from there forty years ago,
the unimagined hidden hoard, struck. The bounty hoisted
up into the blue after a millennium of darkness, I turn
for home and notice, only now, linnets loud in the living hedges,
larks soaring, and how hares have taken the roads as their own.

Roadside Shrine

On a road we'd never normally walk
and which the lockdown has emptied, we explore

the hard shoulder in the direction of our temporary
home, me and my daughter, at eight a relative stranger

to Ireland but growing quickly accustomed. She spots,
on the far side, a break in the hedge for the space of a stone

and points, wondering. I tell her to stay put, and cross
to her first road memorial and break the news

– sixty years on – as gently as I can. Two sisters,
ages eight and twelve, 'accidently killed'.

To soften the blow, we do our own sleuthing
and explaining: weak November light,

where they going or coming home from school,
playing or simply crossing the road,

hand in hand as they are in eternity.
We turn home through a green cathedral

of meeting trees and carry the silence
of that household where everything stopped, ever since.

Other Families' Ghosts

Here we are, dinner in an inherited dining room
painted an unusual green by our host, a girl then,
thirty-five years ago, and hardly ever used
except on occasion and this one delivers a summer
thunderstorm crackling overhead, rain darkening
the fields, shortening the long evening
and rattling window panes.

When I ask after the looming ancestral portraits,
she says, 'all abstemious Quakers to a soul and probably
horrified by the wine and laughter now beneath them'.
The women kindly in bonnets, the men upstanding
and grave, suggesting lives not filled with fun,
and we settle on one wistful one and his romantic
askance, but she's forgotten who he was.

We drink a twenty-one-year-old wine that ripened
in the last century, from your *en primeur* stash
that's been lost to the cellar for a few years until
she found the key in the most obvious place.
Driving home, my wife puts it: 'If that cellar was ours,
you'd have prised the lock or long broken in.'

Wheatear

A last dander down the barren and treeless
peninsula of Lamb's Head which always puts
me in mind of Amorgos and not much birdlife
until a Wheatear pirouetting on rocks
and outlining itself against green Atlantic
and blue sky, its weak song proclaiming
it has been adrift too long on this inclement
island and will return soon to southern Africa.
Much like ourselves who this year have had
a surfeit of the island, and it is time
to turn our prow south and head for home.

Most Appealing Eyes

Adorable Leamington, our inherited black lab named after the royal
spa town for whatever reason by your first set of owners,
and which we quickly abbreviated to 'Lemmy'. Reluctant
  guard dog
but eminent family pet and legendary sleeper on lawns, your
  black coat
assiduously sucked up the sun and just occasionally, having
  had enough,

you'd throw yourself with a heavy thud in the shade of the veranda,
or join with Angel, your sprightlier golden-retriever
  companion,
in the search for phantom bones; diggers and destroyers of
  garden beds.
And while neither dog ever fetched anything, in twilight, their
  nutty half-hour
was made up of pretend scraps and fights our cats
  superciliously stared upon.

Originally 'rescue dogs', we were your third set of owners, and
  had you
for five years, an eternity for our daughter. Who, despite your
  greying
jowls, once insisted on entering you for the local dog
  competition,
a prospect more shire county than Shona in Harare. You
  sauntered off
with a rosette for 'Most Appealing Eyes', a category that was news

to us, and with enough treats to last an age; a tartan dog-
    blanket quickly
shredded and tubs of biscuits, gravy and even doggy *boerewors*.
When Covid came, pets in care, we left for home for four months,
and while summer appeared in Ireland, winter was harsh in Harare.
On our return, Lemmy was effusive, unsteady but tail-wagging.

The following week with friends over, we sat on the veranda
    while the girls
played on swings and Lemmy lay close by, content perhaps
    that laughter
had returned to the dark evenings. Next morning, shortly after
    sunrise,
he lay stretched out and asleep forever, on the lawn. We placed
    him within
our walls and under the flame tree and the leaves he liked
    rustle in.

Punch Rock

for Kerry Wallace

The only irritant
on this pristine morning
as I sit out sipping
black Tanganda tea
with a hunk of submerged
garden lemon in a hand-
thrown cerulean blue
and white porcelain cup;
is the unidentifiable
small brown bird
flitting among emerald
Acacia canopies
sweeping downwards
to a brimming dam.

An Achill Island Icon

after a photograph by Sean Cannon

A gift from you, a year or two before our marriage there,
its framed form has been with us from Dublin, Maynooth, Yangon
and now Harare, and invariably over our desk. Something the eye
is drawn to, its setting has always seemed remote, unattainable,
even when at home. An immense evening, two black snouts of
    mountain

nose the sea and one has won by a head, and between them a bay,
a dark and discernible strand and a few atolls or stepping stones
flung out on the sea. But before this island's *fin del mondo*
and its most westerly spur – Keem Bay's clam embrasure…
And the whole scene engulfed in fog, a witch's overflowing broth

that disappears features. Way beyond twilight, the sun long bolted
and above the darkening layer of cloud and mist,
is a washed-out, Artic yellow; no rich amber or roseate aftermath,
it might even be close to midnight. In the steaming laundry
that was Yangon, one evening I examined a mote in the
    foregrounded sea,

and what I'd always imagined was a static buoy was a boat
    putting out to sea,
night-fishing or some other rendezvous. On another slope, defined
by the light of one household, is forever an evening like another;
the preparation of food, the radio on in the background, or a clock
ticking away a nondescript day and the time, to turn in.

Sunshine

for Afric McGlinchey

I misread your text
'Make the most of the Zim sunshine' as
'Make a moat of the Zim sunshine'
… the Japanese have an expression
that one must build the moat
before one builds the castle,
and I'll do both.

Vides ut alta

after Horace's Ode I:IX

See the whitened peak of Soracte
with its skirt of woods straining
under the white burden,
and falling streams all halt in ice.

Thaw out the cold by stockpiling
logs on the hearth, Thaliarchus,
and liberally decant a decent
four-year-old Sabine wine from its jar.

Leave all else to the gods.
They can still the winds that battle
over the bubbling sea and calm
the commotion raging between
ancient cypresses and ash trees.

Avoid worrying about tomorrow
and what the future sends, write
it off as profit and be open to love
and dancing while you still can,

and green youth rebuffs grey.
Make for the parks and city squares
and soft whispers at appointed times
invariably as dusk falls.

And laughter unbidden from a bower
reveals a girl hiding there,
and a token might be snatched from her wrist
or her coyly resisting finger.

Found Poem/Poet

Sterichorus originally called Tisias
flourished around 550 BC in Sicily,
a Greek lyric poet who wrote

in the Doric dialect, the inventor
of the horse and the stag fable
who had many imitators,

including Horace.
Was probably the first
to compose an epithalamium

but lost his sight
for writing invectives
against Helen of Troy,

then, weirdly after writing
a palinode,
it miraculously returned.

His poems became
sweeter and swan-like
as he approached death.

Of his twenty-six books,
all are lost, only fragmentary
papyri survive.

Hoist sails and gather the scorching gulf winds

a translation

Pearl of the ocean. Star of the West:
beautiful Cuba, your brilliant sky
and how the veil of dark night crosses it
like my brow clouding with sorrow.

I'm leaving, the determined crew
about their business will soon wrench
me from my native earth.
Hoist sails and gather the scorching gulf winds.

Farewell, happy home, beloved Eden,
whatever is in your fates
your sweet name will always ease my ear.

¡Adiós! The tall candle already sizzles,
the anchor's raised and the vessel clears,
takes to the waves and plies silently.

Gertrudis Gómez de Avellaneda (1814–1873)

Myrrha

Having fled the bed of her father,
a game all the family can play
but a crime nonetheless
and not without its warnings,

from her own conscience to the horror
of her nursemaid who turned complicit
or the owls unearthly screeching
when night was missing her fires.

Nine months of wandering shame,
exhausted, she halted in the perfumed
place of Saba, hardly able to carry
the weight of her womb.

Pleading to the heavens
that she didn't want life on earth
or, by passing below, death.
'Refuse me these, change my form.'

As she spoke, the very earth crept
over her feet, roots sprung from under
her cracked toenails, bones became wood
and her marrow flowed with sap.

Arms thus to branches and fingers to twigs,
her alabaster skin gnarled and bunched
to form bark. The tree soon encompassed
her pregnant belly and pendulous breasts

growing toward her neck. She plunged
her head in the trunk of encroaching bark.
Myrrha's emotions were lost with her body
but she continues to weep honoured tears.

Resin distilled from the bark carries her name.

Fireflies

New Year's Eve, 2020

Just ourselves, the musketeers, up in the Vumba mountains
our regular go-to refugee, where there's little to do
and we find ourselves in the almost abandoned Botanical Gardens.

Yesterday, Cyclone Chalane confined us to barracks. All the way
from Madagascar it strengthened in the Mozambique Channel
but, by land, dissipated to a full day of dreary downpour.

All we had to look out on was a row of mountains appearing
and disappearing between waves of rain and beyond them,
lay mythically, Mozambique.

On emerging this afternoon, the high roads all strewn with the bark
of gum trees and minor mud-slides, mountains cast off in the
    distance
with mists heaving and shrouding in some oriental aftermath.

Once the area's showpiece attraction, the Gardens now deserted
and its fringes and great trees have the demeanour of a broken-
down demesne at home; an interior of rainforest where every leaf

is dripping and yesterday's streams run wild. That Japanese aspect
of gardens, borrowing local scenery, has aggrandised a good part
of the neighbouring country's terrain as magnificent backdrop.

No neat lawn edges here, no raked gravel, no proper pruning
since independence, a Rhodesian wheelbarrow shimmied
into a dead-end footpath has rusted into the ground.

In five years here, I've grown to prefer this abandonment.
I follow the rising red-earth lane, hoping for a further view
and come to a kraal of worker's cottages and silence in their yard.

Truly the fag end of the year and my perennial habit of finding
myself on successive New Year's Eves in places voided of people.
So many have not seen this year out: a beloved aunt

who, thousands of miles from here, I see waving
to her son from a window, and in that knowledge.
Mist closes in and even a chill as I catch up with my girls

by the car at twilight, returning to our *Cloudlands* cottage
on the mountainside, to a simple meal and wine.
Thinking, not voicing, that we would not want it

any other way and we'll have retired long before midnight,
when our daughter calls us out to the garden
that has filled with fireflies, that will do for fireworks.

French Toast

On the culinary front, my father's grim
childhood threw up a few gems,
he made a great stew with the occasional
amuse bouche of cigarette ash,
and French toast to die for.

In my fifty-third year, under 'things to do' –
I wrote 'perfect French Toast',
but didn't get round to trying it
in a year where I never cooked
so much in all my life.

Until the year turned, I finally cracked
a few eggs, beating them with milk,
brown sugar and a teaspoon
of cinnamon; letting the sourdough
soak it all up.

Despite having none of the required
accoutrements – Golden Syrup
with that lion from the childhood tin
– we add local acacia honey instead,
and my daughter gives the toast

the thumbs up. Turning ten this year,
the same span since your departure,
and the French toast worth waiting for.

A Ford Prefect in Franschhoek

Evening, and before entering the dark
and ancient wine cellar, Johan introduces us to Suzy,
his rather vicious ostrich but later produces its blown egg
for our daughter; and then cursorily to his collection
of antique cars and, unexpectedly under an awning,

I'm confronted by a perfect black Ford Prefect.
Last seen rusting into the grass of my grandparents' paddock
circa mid 1970s, Longford. I see it still, in the long grass
as if incongruously abandoned by a bunch of mobsters,
having leapt off its broad runner boards to disappear

down the lane to the disappearing turlough.
Its algaed windows and doors rusted shut, conspiring
to conceal the car's inner mystery until, one summer,
a cousin lobbed a stone through the back window
shattering the bottle green glass and releasing
a leathery smell, as if from a time capsule.

An African Hoopoe for Derek Mahon

I liked your lack of sentimentality, your gruff cosmopolitanism
which concealed a certain shyness, that we both knew.
On the day I heard you'd died (which was not the day you died),
an African Hoopoe appeared on our scorched-earth lawn.
You'd have been surprised at how a bird so exotic in the field guide
should appear so dainty and small in close up, disappearing
among the ochreous earth and straw-coloured grass
matching its plumage, bill probing and weaving its way.

Now our garden waits for the impending rains to turn
the parched patches, believe me, into one luminous green baize.
In five years of garden surveillance, King Solomon's emissary
has hardly ever graced us and I see you now, in your Kinsale eyrie,
binos scanning the road and the sea, consoled, while still on
    the island,
you stood as far away from Belfast as was possible. I send you
    this Hoopoe,
Derek, from landlocked Zim. Its busy bill and retracted head-
    crest appearing
as a quill, dipping itself into the inkpot of our soon regenerating
    lawn.

At Altamont

Anything at Altamont?
A thought of Ovid, the lake
and the old lady and workman
on a punt, in all weathers,
and for months dredging
the lake with their bare hands
pulling up weeds
and god knows what,
not since its excavation
during the famine.
Her bravura and 'devil may care'
and the incessant rain, hardly
ever putting pause to the work,
and sometimes the beauty,
the dripping beauty of the gardens,
where everything inherited is overgrown.

The dream of home from a great distance

Sometimes the daydream of returning,
taking the plunge and settling somewhere new
in the home country.
                              Half-heartedly,
I click on counties like Leitrim, Roscommon,
Longford and Westmeath,

which have always had a peculiar and singular
allure, and dream my misanthropic dream
scattered there on detached
                              'farmhouse'
or 'cottage' categories, and peruse silent movies
of loss, damp and dissolution.

                     A marble-topped table
in an empty room of formal stripped wallpaper.
Another, where a fireplace is removed,

                              stolen or remembered,
and the remains of successive crows' nests
fallen through chimneys to fan out on floors.

                              An overcoat,
still hangs on the back of a door and the shoulders
it once graced are surely in clay now.

                     Plays of light
on empty interiors and one house populated
by family photos, children sitting on sunlit steps
                              in a 1970s sepia.
Gardens green, I'll grant you, but more often
inclining to a low horizon. A bungalow,

                                        sits in so much rain
to shine like the new button, were it not for
the roof reflecting dark and ominous skies.

                                An interior
of a cowshed bearing all the hallmarks
of a handyman, but the centred single chair

                                        sends a shudder,
the imagined interrogation and a sentence
administered in perfect silence.

Let's get lost

Let's get crossed off everybody's list
— sung by Chet Baker

Who'd have thought from such beginnings
still together now after twenty years, despite two earthquakes
early on which had roles in bringing us together.
And not to mention that tsunami or its aftermath
that sent you scurrying off again. In the fourth year
of our marriage we choose to circle the globe
with all its consequences as if to make a vow
of restlessness or simply add to the sum of years
on the road. With our only daughter barely walking
we flitted first to toddler-friendly Burma
and, after free elections, thence to Zim …
A few coups d'états later, we sit on the veranda
and exhale to evening shadows lengthening on the grass,
I reach for your hand, hoping we never settle.

Rain Storks

Always preferred 'Rain stork' to 'Abdim's stork'
since, despite summer, they bring the rains,
and this year the most bounteous in years.
Congregating, almost huddled on the open veld,
old men nodding in overcoats, gathered for a farewell.

Bicycle Thieves

i.m. Samuel Menashe (1925–2011)

Lunch in The Loeb Boathouse,
the winter sun enlivening the lake
in Central Park, your 'living room'
as you called it, and all the waiters
fussing over you and you just fussing,
but happy your *Collected* had *finally*
found an English publisher like your first
back in '61 and you, condemned in between
to being 'the most famous unfamous poet
in the world'. And my unease at you
turning up at my reading the night before
and why hadn't I told you I was in town?
But among the darkened auditorium,
you made your august presence known.
After lunch in our shared taxi uptown,
I was gathering to say something
when you spotted a matinee showing
of Vittorio De Sica's classic, *Bicycle Thieves,*
and commanded the cab driver to pull aside,
with just enough time to catch
one of the most marvellous movies
of the century and would I join you?
A quick embrace, you shuffled across
the street and the last I ever saw of you.

Summer Home Fires Burning

Whether for instance on a holiday, it is better to revisit or explore.
— Freya Stark

Each summer of your childhood abroad
we took a house on the slopes –
same place as your mother's childhood summers
while our house and others on the steep hills
filled with family and friends,
and summers were Chekhovian.

An almost-fantasy place of sea, rockpools
and mountains, smooth and jagged islands
on the horizon, changeable weather and skies
in which to earth ourselves. And since grandparents
had fled this earthly coop, here was a place to return to.

No summer the same; and once, engulfed
by a bank of fog that sat for four days -
a temporary ice-age with blooms of dew
on estuarine sands. We walked the ghostly
dunes, when three figures on horseback
emerged, as if from a dream.

Then on the fifth day the veil lifted:
one morning a plume of smoke
belched and searched seawards
as if from a tiny volcano,
a family leaving their holiday house
had tipped ashes outside

and the smouldering began.
All that week of your eighth summer
we watched from our eyrie across the bay,
the treeless peninsula and its heather smouldering
and evenings of wind whipping up the flames.
And for once, we wished for rain.

Distant Accordion Music

*I myself am ok until I hear some Irish music, specifically someone
playing a slow air and then I'm hooked like a seven-hundred-pound
carp in a Chinese pond.*
— Macdara Woods

Lining up for my overnight plane
– that was to take me through days
of staggered delays and an unscheduled
and 'complimentary' afternoon
in an Addis Ababa hotel whose myriad shades
of brown inspired the impromptu
tourist in me to wander round such
sights as St. George's cathedral
where the emperor was coronated —
        my phone rang and it was you
whom I'd visited in hospital days earlier
and, not knowing then, I'd never see
you in the flesh again and I could hear
no voice and held the phone closer
to my better ear and then faintly,
among destination announcements,
distant accordion music
(traditional and being channelled
from an even more distant radio
as if someone had stepped out
of the room, the playing elsewhere)
ancient but jaunty and about
to step off a coverage cliff,
I never did get to return
your wordless call.

Are you a farmer?

Taking off my *veldskoens*
at Robert Gabriel Mugabe International Airport

when the security lady asks me,
'Are you a farmer?' to which I shake my head.

'Those are farmer's boots,' she points.

Egg-fried Rice

For my daughter's school lunch today, cooking egg fried rice
and you, Maki, shuffled right into my head, from thirty years past.
That day when you needed an 'emergency' English teacher
for interminable conversation classes that would last until evening
in the Kyoto suburbs, in your private English school adjoining
    your house.
And on my one day off, I may have taken your call lying on
    the futon,
and off I went, like a doctor on call but by commuter train.
You offered me lunch before the students arrived, but demurred
you were a terrible cook, an unusual declaration even then.
And yes, I was fine with *hashi* and ate the delicious yellowed
    and green,
spring-onioned rice. You mentioned it was a way of using leftovers,
and it has remained with me since, become part of my everyday,
and what has become of you Maki? Middle-aged then and
    with a grown-up
family, your wide smile eternally delivering your impromptu
    creation.

Islander

We are leaving the island on a Sunday in winter
and the bar to its solitary drinker, who has just arrived
in and asks, 'are we off?' He retired home, here,
after a working life in Birmingham, busy bachelorhood,
men's clubs and friends he could drink and play cards with.

Here, it is only the wind and the rain on that wind
and no one ever drops by. I mention he's retired
to a beautiful place and he says, 'you've never spent
a winter on it. Go now, I won't delay ye newlyweds
and good luck, you're both off to a better place'.

Kermanshah

for Kathy Bond Stewart,
at Doris Lessing's childhood farm on her birthday, 22 October, 2020.

If only we had known the real history of that area
— Doris Lessing

My cartographer friend found it –
and sent over a map with marked-off
boundaries of the estate in the shape
of an upside-down church
which might have amused you.

Not far from flyblown Banket
but a distance nonetheless on a red-earth
road and one you'd often trod
as a disaffected teenager, to a tapering
turn and another dirt road up a kopje

where your 'house on a hill' stood.
Of course, the family living there now
had heard some rumour of you, but vague
and irrelevant as any history of white farmers.
They gathered at the back of the bungalow

which has long replaced your family's
'pole and dagga' arrangement and sadza
cooked in the yard under a low thatched roof.
The elegant daughter nominated to accompany us,
more curious than chaperone, tagged along

while we walked the fringes of the farm's summit
and drank in the immense landscape that haunted
your entire life. Your house 'raised high on its eminence',

and in the centre of this vast basin, bounded by mountains,
north to the Ayrshire Hills over ridges, vleis

and two 'named' rivers, and to the east,
the Great Dyke which earlier, I'd driven over
from Harare, and whose crystalline blues
and purples ignited with the sun's monotonous progress.
As a child you slept with your bedroom door open

on the night sky and majesty of it all. Later wondering
how it might have helped your lost mother to know
that the Great Dyke connected to the Rift Valley
and was a spur to the Indian ocean, an escape route
to dream upon and draw you out of your despair.

Causalities from the War, everything failed here
for your parents, from your father's farming schemes;
various crops to a litany of livestock, dead on a biblical scale,
and eventually giving way to gold prospecting.
You sometimes spied upon them in the cauldron

of the day as they lay abed, fitfully napping,
flanked on either side by ill-fitting dentures in tumblers
of water, their bothersome teeth having been removed
before leaving England. You abandoned 'the district'
as a teenager, having all you needed, and rarely

darkened the door or the district again, and in time
your parents too, for the Salisbury suburbs.
Before our leaving, the mother of the house proudly
showed us a little orchard and a strip of beans
and marigolds shored up against the searing October sun,

perhaps a Lessing legacy of sorts. I ask her
what is the farm now called, and she answers,
'Kermanshah, we call it Kermanshah.'

Keenagh

Before then, a series of drivers in Burma who came and went,
supplied like unsuitable nannies until the last, Koye.
When I took to driving with an unlicenced gusto,
I was almost fifty, and then in Africa, zipping round the 'burbs
on school, swimming and playdate runs, which eventually
opened to epic cross-country and off-road driving
or the thousand kilometres it took, to Vic Falls
and the Caprivi Strip. Sometimes toying with plans
for driving all the way home, I'd screen saved it on Maps,
Harare to Drogheda, as if the latter could ever be called home
again, but seven days solid driving without a breather
and a trajectory through the Congo, might not have augured well.
The car sold and the ex-patriate life and home packed away,
a nomadic summer at home ensued. Every time, I sat behind
     the wheel,
it was only African roads, superimposed, on what I could see.
Leaving Leitrim for the Vita Nuova of Limerick, to drive down
through the middle country with the family ensconced, during
     a day
of teeming and relentless rain on unknown roads.
Until, passing through a tiny village, I glimpsed a looming pub,
and in that instant, recognised the locus of a memory I'd taken
     for a dream,
such was its mundanity and repetition; simply a child in my
     father's halted
Worsley, mid 1970s, with my elderly black-suited and trilby-
     hatted grandfather,
and across the road, that very pub – what was the occasion,
     a farewell,
a rendezvous or had we broken bread there? And now, no one
     to ask.

Enough to get us to Marondera

An adopted saying in our household,
meaning; on an empty fuel tank there's enough
fumes to get us home, and when I said this
at a filling station near Limerick,
your tears welled up.

Boxed Set

i.m. David Palacious (1967–2023)

> *Between them Hugo and Shakespeare have exhausted every*
> *subject. Originality is no longer possible – even in sin.*
> — Oscar Wilde

In your Havana boyhood
when you scampered home
victoriously with the coveted
second-hand, five volumes
of Hugo's *Los Miserables,*

your father secretly
and lovingly set about
making a wooden case
for them, not a bookcase
or even a double shelf

for additional finds,
but a polished open box
to corral only Hugo's five volumes.
As if that was the sum total,
and Victor Hugo might concur,
of all the books you'd ever require.

Corncrake

for Paul Masterson

Mr Keegan in primary school back in the seventies declared
we'd be lucky to hear the corncrake's call in our lifetimes,
such was its scarcity. But I did, twenty-something years ago
on Boffin and accepted its benighted blessing.
Back again this year in May and, from the uncut meadow
in front of the Harbour Lights bookshop, I heard its call
if you could call it that. Now our daughter gets to carry it on
and dreams of its winging return to the Congo and Southern Africa
in winter, its washer board riff, its 'crex crex' in Linnaean Latin.

'Kermanshah', *p. 68:*
Doris Lessing was born in Kermanshah, Iran in 1919 to British parents. In 1925 her family moved to Southern Rhodesia (now Zimbabwe) to farm near a town called Banket, about 100 km northeast of Harare (then Salisbury). They called the farm Kemanshah.

Milton Keynes UK
Ingram Content Group UK Ltd.
UKHW010638290424
441924UK00005B/377

9 781915 629296